DOWNSIZING

The Surprising Key to Financial Freedom and a Life That Fits You

Rosemarie R Williams

Dedication

For everyone who's ever looked around and realized that "having it all" wasn't what they really wanted after all.

This book is for the brave souls who are ready to trade busy for balanced, clutter for clarity, and the weight of more for the peace of enough.

And for those still finding the courage to let go— may these pages remind you that what you release isn't loss.

It's the beginning of freedom.

Acknowledgments

Writing this book was a journey of its own—a process of releasing, refining, and returning to what matters most.

To the people who have walked alongside me—thank you. To my readers, clients, and community who've shared your stories and struggles so openly: you are the heartbeat behind these pages. Every insight, every breakthrough, every "aha" moment I've written about began with someone like you, daring to take that first small step toward simplicity.

To my friends and family who reminded me to pause, breathe, and live what I was writing—you've been my mirror and my anchor. Thank you for believing in this message even when the world shouted "more."

And to everyone who has ever sat surrounded by too much—stuff, noise, pressure—and wondered if peace was still possible: it is.

You are proof that freedom isn't something you find. It's something you *create*.

Copyright Page

Downsizing: The Surprising Key to Financial Freedom and a Life That Fits You © 2025 by Rosemarie Williams

All rights reserved. No part of this publication may be reproduced, stored in a retrieval system, or transmitted in any form or by any means—electronic, mechanical, photocopying, recording, or otherwise—without prior written permission from the author, except for brief quotations used in reviews or articles.

For information, contact: Rosemarie Williams at rosemariespage@outlook.com

https://www.amazon.com/author/rosemariewilliams

Cover Design: Rosemarie R Williams

Interior Design: Rosemarie R Williams

ISBN: 9798333041852

Imprint: Independently published

Disclaimer

This book is intended for informational and motivational purposes only. The author is not a financial advisor, therapist, or licensed counselor. The ideas and suggestions contained herein reflect personal experience and research designed to inspire and support personal growth and financial mindfulness.

Readers are encouraged to consult qualified professionals before making major financial or lifestyle decisions. Publishers' and author assume no responsibility for any actions taken based on the contents of this book.

Every effort has been made to ensure the accuracy of information at the time of publication. All names, characters, and stories used in illustrative examples are either fictitious or used with permission. Any resemblance to actual persons, living or deceased, is purely coincidental.

Turning the Key
Your Guide Through Downsizing

INTRODUCTION "When Having It All Starts to Cost Too Much"..................2

Chapter 1: The High Cost of Having It All: Why more stuff doesn't mean more security.................5

Chapter 2: Decluttering Your Financial Mindset You can't simplify your space without simplifying your headspace.................14

Chapter 3: The Freedom Audit: The first step to freedom is knowing what's holding you hostage.................22

Chapter 4: The Money–Home Connection Your space tells your financial story.................32

Chapter 5: The Emotional Price Tag Every item you keep carries a story — and a cost.................42

Chapter 6: Debt Detox Clearing financial clutter to make room for freedom.................51

Chapter 7: The True Definition of Wealth It's not what you own. It's what you have the freedom to experience.................61

Chapter 8: Designing a Life That Fits You can't live your best life in someone else's blueprint.................70

Chapter 9: The Ripple Effect of Less: How simplifying changes relationships, productivity, and self-worth. ... **78**

Chapter 10: Sustaining Freedom Keeping simplicity alive in a world that sells complexity. **89**

Conclusion: Freedom Is the New Rich **99**

Reader's Reflection & Discussion Guide............... **105**

Resources & Recommended Reading Because freedom doesn't end on the last page. **109**

Recommended Reading: Living Light & Financial Clarity **111**

INTRODUCTION

"When Having It All Starts to Cost Too Much"

There comes a point when the math stops adding up. Not in your bank account, but in your spirit.

You realize that somewhere between the promotions, the upgrades, and the "just one more thing," life got crowded. Your calendar filled. Your house filled. Your mind filled. But your joy? That somehow got smaller.

We call it progress. But what if it's just noise?

For years, I believed that more meant better. A bigger home, nicer car, a calendar packed with commitments—it all looked like success on the outside. But somewhere along the way, I started feeling tired in a way that sleep couldn't fix. I had surrounded myself with everything I thought I wanted, yet I still felt like something was missing.

And then one day, while reorganizing a closet that refused to close, it hit me: I wasn't short on space. I was short on *clarity*.

That moment changed everything.

I began to see how "too much" had crept into every corner of my life—not just in what I owned, but in how I thought and how I spent. Every extra item, every unnecessary bill, every "yes" I didn't mean was costing me something: peace, energy, and time I could never get back.

So, I started letting go.

Not recklessly, but consciously. One drawer. One bill. One boundary at a time.

And in that process, I discovered something no one talks about enough: downsizing isn't about living with less—it's about living with purpose.

This book isn't a manual for minimalists. It's a guide for real people who want their lives to make sense again. It's for anyone who's ever looked around and thought, *"Why am I working so hard to sustain things that don't even fulfill me?"*

Inside these pages, we'll explore how your space, money, and mindset all intertwine—and how simplifying one naturally heals the others. You'll meet stories of people who downsized not out of loss, but out of liberation. And you'll find tools to help you design a life that fits *you*, not the other way around.

Because the truth is, "having it all" only matters if what you have brings peace.

And freedom—real, lasting freedom—starts the moment you stop chasing and start choosing.

Let's begin there.

CHAPTER 1

The High Cost of Having It All

Chapter 1

Why more stuff doesn't mean more security

The Illusion of More

Let's be honest — most of us grew up believing that success looked like *more*.

A bigger house meant you were "moving up." A newer car meant you were "doing well." More clothes, gadgets, subscriptions, and square footage all meant you were *winning at life*.

And for a while, it feels good. You walk into that new home, run your hand along the countertop, and think, *I've made it*.

But somewhere between the upgraded appliances and the second car payment, something shifts. The sense of pride quietly turns into pressure. The very things that were meant to make life easier start owning the hours of your day and the peace in your mind.

This is how **lifestyle inflation** sneaks in — not as a deliberate decision, but as a series of tiny "yeses" we rarely question.

- "Just one upgrade."
- "Just one renovation."
- "Just one small payment."

Before you know it, you're not living the dream — you're financing it.

The 'Just One Upgrade' Spiral

It's never the big purchase that traps you. It's the chain reaction that follows it. You buy the bigger home… then you need the better furniture to fill it.

You buy the new SUV… and suddenly the old tools in your garage look outdated.

Each decision fuels the next, and without realizing it, you've built an entire lifestyle around maintaining appearances instead of maintaining peace.

We rarely ask, *"Do I actually need this?"* because the world around us keeps whispering, *"You deserve it."*

But what we often deserve most is *breathing room* — not another payment plan.

Emotional Triggers: Status, Scarcity, and Social Proof

At its core, our obsession with "more" isn't really about greed — it's about emotion.

Three invisible triggers tend to drive most of our unnecessary spending and accumulation:

1. **Status:** We use stuff to measure worth — to feel competent, admired, or "caught up." But validation through possessions is a bottomless pit. The more we chase it, the emptier we feel when the applause fades.

2. **Scarcity:** We buy things out of fear — the fear of missing out, of not being prepared, of losing control. "What if I

need it later?" becomes the anthem of every overstuffed closet.

3. **Social Proof:** When everyone around us is upgrading, we assume it's normal. Keeping up doesn't even feel like comparison anymore — it feels like survival.

But here's the truth: **owning more doesn't mean you have more security.**

It often means you've created more obligations disguised as achievements.

What It Really Costs You

Every possession in your life has three price tags:

Money.
Time.
Energy.

You pay for it when you buy it, you pay for it when you maintain it, and you pay for it every time you think about it.
That extra room? It needs furniture, heating, and cleaning. That second car? It needs insurance, registration, and repairs. Even digital clutter has a cost — endless emails, subscriptions, and "free trials" that drain attention and auto-renew on your credit card.

These are the **hidden financial leaks** most people overlook:

- Maintenance and repairs on things rarely used.

- Insurance on items that depreciate faster than we can enjoy them.

- Storage units filled with "someday" items that silently siphon $100+ a month.
- The biggest one: the *time* spent managing it all — the hours spent earning money to maintain what we barely use.

When you zoom out, it's not just about money — it's about what your possessions are *costing you in peace*.

The Three Currencies

If you strip everything down, every choice in life costs one (or more) of these currencies:

1. **Money** – The tangible cost.
2. **Time** – The hours you trade to earn it or maintain it.
3. **Energy** – The mental bandwidth you lose thinking about it.

When these currencies are unbalanced, life starts to feel heavier than it should.

The secret to reclaiming balance — and ultimately, *freedom* — lies in what I call the **Freedom Equation**:

Space + Simplicity = Peace × Prosperity

It's simple, but profound.

When you create space — physically, financially, emotionally — and pair it with simplicity, your peace multiplies. Your prosperity isn't just about money anymore. It's about time, health, joy, and purpose.

You don't have to downsize your dreams — just the distractions that keep you from living them.

We all know this equation sounds good on paper — but what happens when life tempts us with more instead of less? When success, convenience, or comfort quietly start cluttering the very freedom we're chasing? Sometimes, it takes losing our balance to see what truly matters.

That's exactly what happened to Chris and Dana.

Real Talk Story:

The Upgrade That Downgraded Their Life

Meet Chris and Dana.

They were the picture of progress — two solid careers, two kids, and a cozy starter home they'd outgrown. Or so they thought. When Dana got a promotion, they decided it was time for "the next step." A bigger home in a better neighborhood.

The first few months felt magical. Everything was new — the open-concept kitchen, the spa-like bathroom, the walk-in closets. But soon, the costs began to stack up: higher mortgage, higher utilities, HOA fees, new furniture to fill the larger space, and endless maintenance.

They noticed something odd — the more space they had, the less time they spent enjoying it.

Chris started working longer hours to cover expenses. Dana took on extra projects. They joked about "house poor" life at dinner, but underneath, the stress was real.

One evening, while folding laundry in a house they barely lived in, Dana looked around and said, "We thought this was freedom. But I think we just bought a prettier cage."

That moment hit hard — and it's one that many of us quietly recognize.

We chase comfort, but comfort built on consumption becomes a trap. The dream home, the bigger car, the constant upgrades — they often lead not to freedom, but to fatigue.

Action Step: Calculate Your Real Cost of Comfort

Let's bring this home (pun intended).

If you want to see the true cost of "having it all," try this simple exercise:

1. **List your top 5 recurring expenses** — mortgage or rent, car payment, insurance, subscriptions, storage, etc.
2. **Add them up for the month.**
3. **Divide that number by your hourly wage.**

Now ask yourself:

"How many hours of my life each month do I trade just to sustain this lifestyle?"

That's your **Real Cost of Comfort.**

Once you see how much life you're exchanging for things that don't always bring joy or peace, you'll never look at "stuff" the same way again.

Closing Thought

Having it all isn't about accumulation — it's about alignment. When your life begins to reflect your values instead of your ego, that's when true richness takes root.

You don't need to own more to become more.

You just need to make space for what genuinely matters — time with those you love, moments that spark joy, and quiet pauses that let you breathe it all **in**. Because that's where fulfillment really lives.

CHAPTER 2
THE MINDSET SHIFT

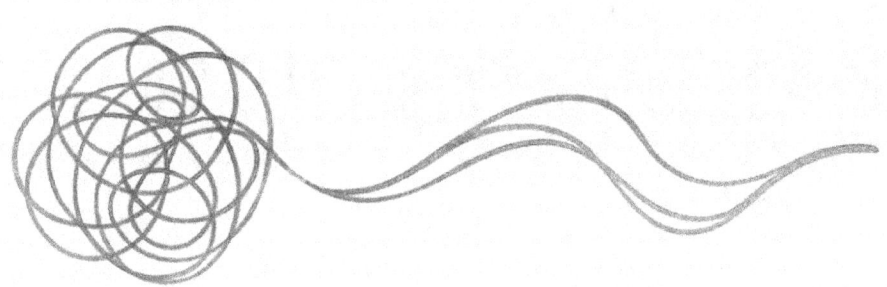

Chapter 2

Decluttering Your Financial Mindset

You can't simplify your space without simplifying your headspace.

The Stories We Tell About Money

Before we can declutter a single drawer, we have to declutter the beliefs that built it.

Because let's face it — every purchase, every collection, and every "I might need this someday" is just a reflection of the stories we tell ourselves about what we value, what we fear, and what we deserve.

Some of us grew up with the mantra: "Money doesn't grow on trees."

Others were taught the opposite: "If you've got it, flaunt it."

Both stories create clutter — one in the form of deprivation, the other in the form of excess.

Our *money mindset* shapes how we spend, save, and stress. It decides whether we chase "more" out of fear of lack or buy things to fill emotional gaps we've never named. Before you can create financial freedom, you have to know which voice is really running the show.

Your Money Story: Where It All Began

Every person has what I call a **financial origin story** — the emotional blueprint we formed long before we ever had a paycheck.

Maybe you watched your parents fight over bills, and money became synonymous with anxiety.

Maybe you grew up in a household that equated success with status symbols.

Maybe you've always been the helper — the one who gives generously, even when your own account is running on empty.

Those early experiences don't just disappear. They hide in your habits:

- The guilt you feel when spending on yourself.
- The urge to upgrade every time you feel "less than."
- The comfort you find in buying, even when you know it's temporary.

The truth is, money isn't emotional — *we are.*

It's a mirror, showing us what we value, what we fear, and where we still seek validation.

Reflection Prompt:

"What did I learn about money growing up — and how is that lesson showing up in my life today?"

Bonus Thought:

Our habits with money often mirror how we treat ourselves: do we hoard, overspend, neglect, or invest?

The Emotional Spending Trap

We live in a world that sells emotion disguised as convenience. When life feels stressful, we buy things that promise relief: the cozy blanket, the online course, the gadget that claims to make life "simpler." But in reality, emotional spending rarely fixes what's broken — it just buries it under packaging.

Common emotional triggers that lead to financial clutter:

- **Boredom:** "I deserve a little excitement."
- **Stress:** "I need something to take the edge off."
- **Loneliness:** "It feels good to get a package in the mail."
- **Comparison:** "They have it, I should too."

Here's the thing: spending feels like *control*.

When we're overwhelmed, making a purchase gives us an instant sense of relief — but it's a false one. The peace fades, and the guilt creeps in. That's the emotional hangover of modern consumerism.

Try This: "Pause Before Purchase" Mini Exercise

Next time you're about to buy something, stop and ask yourself three quick questions:

1. What emotion am I feeling right now?
2. Will this purchase solve the emotion or distract from it?
3. How will I feel about this choice next week?

If it won't matter in seven days, it probably doesn't deserve your energy — or your dollars.

Scarcity vs. Sufficiency: A Mindset Shift

Here's a radical idea: what if *you already have enough?* Not "barely enough to get by," but *enough to build from.*

The scarcity mindset whispers, "There isn't enough to go around." The sufficiency mindset replies, "There's enough for me when I use what I have wisely."

Scarcity says, *buy now before it's gone.*

Sufficiency says, *choose what matters most and release the rest.*

When you operate from scarcity, downsizing feels like loss. When you operate from sufficiency, downsizing feels like liberation.

This mental shift is the foundation for every financial transformation that lasts

Because freedom doesn't come from having more — it comes from wanting less.

Mini-Journal Prompt:

"What would my spending look like if I truly believed I already had enough?"

Decluttering the Financial Clutter

We often think of clutter as stuff lying around, but financial clutter hides in plain sight.

It's not just the old receipts or forgotten accounts — it's the weight of decisions we never revisit.

Examples of hidden financial clutter:

- Subscriptions we forgot to cancel.
- Loyalty programs we don't use.
- Bank accounts or credit cards opened "just in case."
- Recurring charges we can't even identify.
- Fear-based "safety nets" that now feel like chains.

Start your cleanout here before you ever touch your closet. Simplify the way money *moves through your life*, and everything else gets lighter.

Quick Exercise: "The Subscription Sweep"

- Print your last month's statement.
- Highlight every recurring charge.
- Circle the ones you *actually use*.
- Cancel one today. Just one. That single act of reclaiming control sends a powerful message to your brain: *I run my life. My bills don't run me.*

From Fear to Freedom

When you start viewing money as a tool — not a scorecard — everything changes.

You stop competing and start creating. You stop apologizing and start aligning.

You realize that financial peace isn't built on earning more; it's built on understanding *why* you spend, and deciding to spend in alignment with who you're becoming.

This is the inner decluttering that sets the stage for everything that follows in this book — because once your mindset shifts from fear to freedom, every decision feels lighter.

Action Step: The "Money Mirror" Exercise

Grab your journal and answer these honestly:

1. When I think about money, the first word that comes to mind is _____.
2. The last time I made a purchase I regretted, what was I really feeling?
3. What would financial peace look and feel like for me — not in theory, but in my actual daily life?

Once you finish, underline any recurring words or patterns. Those are your emotional triggers.

Awareness is the first step toward freedom — because you can't release what you can't see.

Closing Thought

Before you declutter your closet or sell a single item, declutter the story that says your worth depends on what you own. The truth is simpler, quieter, and far more powerful: "You don't need more things to feel secure.

You need more alignment between what you say matters and how you live each day. Because when your choices start reflecting your truth, freedom stops being a dream — it becomes the way you live."

CHAPTER 3
The Freedom Audit

Chapter 3

The first step to freedom is knowing what's holding you hostage

Seeing the Whole Picture

You can't change what you won't look at.

That's where this chapter begins — with the courage to finally face what's weighing you down.

When life feels cluttered, it's tempting to fix what's visible: clean a drawer, pay off a small bill, reorganize a closet. But real transformation begins when you look beneath the surface and see the bigger pattern. The *Freedom Audit* is your map — a way to see where your energy, time, and money are going, and whether they still serve the life you want.

Most people don't realize how much of their daily stress isn't caused by chaos, but by misalignment — the gap between the life they're living and the one they actually want. This chapter helps you bridge that gap.

Auditing Your Life, Not Just Your Stuff

Think of this process as a life inventory.

Not in the sterile, spreadsheet kind of way — but as an honest check-in with yourself.

We're not just talking about physical clutter; we're talking about everything that takes up *space* in your world: your home, your finances, your relationships, your habits, and even your digital life.

When you step back and see your life as a whole system, patterns start to reveal themselves:

- The way your home feels mirrors your inner state.
- The way you spend money mirrors your priorities.
- The way you spend time mirrors what you believe you're worth.

If you feel heavy, scattered, or constantly behind, it's not because you're doing life wrong — it's because your environment and energy are carrying outdated versions of you.

Freedom isn't created through control — it's created through clarity.

The "Too Much" Matrix

Let's get specific

To perform a Freedom Audit, start by identifying where you have "too much" in your life. There are four categories where clutter tends to hide:

1. **Too Much Stuff** – closets, garages, storage units, drawers full of "someday."

2. **Too Many Obligations** – overcommitments, emotional labor, and saying "yes" when you mean "no."

3. **Too Many Expenses** – bills, memberships, or purchases that no longer match your values.

4. **Too Many Distractions** – social media, toxic relationships, and mental noise that steal your focus.

When you label your "too much" zones, you instantly see what's been stealing your peace — often without permission.

Write down one example in each category. Don't judge yourself; this isn't a test, it's a mirror.

The Four Zones of Ownership

Every item, expense, or commitment in your life belongs to one of four zones: **Use, Need, Love, or Obligation.**

1. **Use:** Things that serve a purpose. You interact with them regularly and intentionally.

    Example: The coffee mug you use daily.

2. **Need:** Things that provide stability or safety. You may not use them every day, but they're essential.

    Example: Health insurance, important documents, reliable transportation.

3. **Love:** Things that add beauty, meaning, or joy. They nourish your spirit and reflect your identity.

    Example: A photograph, an heirloom, a book that changed your life.

4. **Obligation:** Things you keep out of guilt, fear, or habit.

    Example: Gifts you never liked, clothes that don't fit, commitments you've outgrown.

The goal isn't to strip your life bare — it's to move as much as possible into the *Use, Need, and Love* zones. Everything else becomes a candidate for release.

The Practical Audit: One Room, One Hour

Start where you are, not where you wish you were.

Most people fail at simplifying because they attack too much at once. The Freedom Audit takes a gentler, more sustainable approach.

Choose **one small space** — a single drawer, shelf, or surface. Set a timer for one hour.

During that hour, ask yourself four questions for every item you touch:

1. Do I use this?
2. Do I need this?
3. Do I love this?
4. Or am I keeping it out of obligation?

Sort items accordingly, and when the timer rings, stop. Don't push for perfection; aim for momentum. The satisfaction of one clear space will give you the energy to tackle the next.

Repeat this method room by room, corner by corner, decision by decision.

Freedom is built in layers.

Beyond the Home: Life Habits and Financial Audit

Once you've practiced the physical audit, apply the same framework to your **habits and spending.**

Ask:

- What do I *use* and what do I *ignore*?
- What do I *need* versus what I've convinced myself I do?
- What do I *love* and what just looks good on paper?
- What am I doing or paying for out of *obligation*?

You may realize your calendar is full of things that don't move you forward.

You may see subscriptions you forgot, or friendships that now drain rather than inspire.

These discoveries aren't failures — they're openings.

Every time you release something that doesn't belong to your current season of life, you reclaim energy for the next one.

Reflection: Questions That Reveal Hidden Clutter

- What part of my life feels most "crowded"?
- Where am I maintaining something out of guilt or fear?
- What do I keep telling myself I'll deal with "later"?
- Which area of my life gives me peace — and why?

Your answers will point directly to the next step in your Freedom Audit.

The Freedom Audit Quick Start Checklist

Use this checklist as your launchpad. The goal isn't to check every box in one day, but to build awareness.

Physical Spaces

- Walk through each room and note what feels heavy, chaotic, or overstuffed.
- Identify one area that would make you feel lighter if simplified.

Finances

- Review your most recent bank or credit card statement.
- Highlight three recurring expenses that no longer align with your current values.

Habits

- Track where your time goes for one day.
- Mark anything that drains more energy than it gives.

Relationships and Commitments

- Reflect on any relationship or responsibility that feels one-sided or forced.
- Ask yourself: if I released this, would I feel guilt or relief?

The more honest you are, the faster the fog clears.

Why Awareness Is Everything

Awareness alone can feel small, but it's powerful. It's the crack in the wall where the light gets in.

Most people try to "fix" their cluttered lives by organizing it better — but organization isn't liberation. It's just tidier captivity. The Freedom Audit helps you see that your external environment is an extension of your internal one.

When you finally see the whole system — how time, money, and space interact — you start to live intentionally instead of reactively. That's the quiet beginning of financial freedom and emotional peace.

Action Step: Your First Freedom Audit

This week, perform your first Freedom Audit using this plan:

1. Pick one physical space (a closet, a drawer, or even your car).
2. Spend one hour sorting items into the four zones: Use, Need, Love, Obligation.
3. Write down any emotions or resistance that surface.
4. Repeat the same audit for one area of your finances — your bank statement, digital subscriptions, or a budget category.
5. Note any patterns that connect the two. (For example, do you overspend in areas tied to emotional clutter?)

When you finish, don't rush to declutter everything. Sit with the clarity. Freedom begins in that pause — in realizing you finally see your life with open eyes.

Closing Thought

Freedom doesn't always arrive with fanfare. Sometimes it starts quietly, in a single hour of honesty.

You'll recognize it the moment you look around and realize the heaviness is gone — that you're finally free from the weight of things, and standing inside a life that feels right.

CHAPTER 4

The Money–Home Connection

Chapter 4

Your space tells your financial story.

When Your House Starts Speaking

If your home could talk, what would it say about your relationship with money?

Would it whisper peace or sigh exhaustion?

Every corner of our home tells a story — not just of what we own, but *why* we own it. Our surroundings quietly reflect our beliefs about safety, success, and self-worth. And often, those beliefs are outdated, inherited, or written by fear.

When you walk into your kitchen, you might see the unspoken story of "I need to be prepared for everything."

Open your closet, and it might tell a story of "Someday I'll fit into that again."

Peek into your garage, and it might quietly confess, "I used to be someone who did that hobby."

Homes are mirrors. They don't lie

They reveal how you spend, how you cope, and how you define comfort.

Downsizing your life isn't just about getting rid of stuff — it's about rewriting the story your space is telling about you.

Every Room Reflects a Relationship with Money

Let's walk through your house, not to critique it, but to listen.

The Kitchen of Abundance (and Excess)

The kitchen often mirrors our relationship with *plenty*. Some kitchens overflow with duplicates — five spatulas, three blenders, and endless storage containers.

It's not greed; it's a subconscious response to fear. We overbuy to avoid ever feeling unprepared again.

Ask yourself:

- What am I trying to make sure I never run out of?
- Where did I learn that running out equals failure?

Shifting from fear-based accumulation to confidence-based preparation is one of the fastest ways to build peace — and save money.

The Living Room of Image

The living room tells the story we want others to believe. It's where the best furniture sits, often purchased to impress more than to enjoy. There's nothing wrong with creating beauty, but when design becomes a disguise for debt or dissatisfaction, the space loses authenticity.

Ask yourself:

- Who am I decorating for?
- Does this room invite real living, or is it just a display?

A peaceful home doesn't need to perform. It needs to *welcome*.

The Bedroom of Avoidance

The bedroom should be a sanctuary — but for many, it's a holding zone for unfinished business: laundry piles, unread books, shopping bags we haven't unpacked. This clutter quietly drains our sense of rest and self-care.

Ask yourself:

- What in this room represents an unmade decision?
- What would peace look like here, not perfection?

The Garage of "Someday"

Garages, basements, and storage units are emotional museums. They're filled with identities we once tried on: the DIY version of ourselves, the hobbyist, the collector, the fixer, the saver.

There's tenderness in those corners — but also stagnation. Holding on too tightly to who we *were* can keep us from funding who we're becoming.

Ask yourself:

- Which of these items reflect a chapter I've already finished?
- What could I gain by releasing this version of me?

How Physical Clutter Creates Financial Clutter

The connection between your environment and your wallet is direct and measurable.

When your space is disorganized, your finances often are too — because both run on energy, clarity, and decision-making.

Think about it:

- Clutter hides what you already own, so you buy duplicates.
- Overstuffed spaces make you avoid certain areas, so you ignore what's broken or overdue.
- A chaotic home lowers focus, making you more likely to chase quick relief through spending.

The emotional weight of "too much" doesn't just sit on your shelves it sits in your budget. Every object you manage requires energy. And energy, just like money, has limits.

Designing an Environment That Reflects Financial Clarity

The good news?

When you intentionally create an environment that mirrors your values, your finances begin to align naturally. You spend less impulsively, because you already feel content. You make smarter choices, because you're not buying to escape discomfort — you're living in a space that supports calm.

Here's how to begin shifting your surroundings from *draining* to *defining*.

1. Simplify Surfaces

A clear countertop or table communicates completion. It says, "I have enough."

Choose one surface — your nightstand, kitchen counter, or desk — and make it a clutter-free zone.

That single act of visual calm ripples into mental calm, which influences spending habits more than most realize.

2. Curate, Don't Decorate

Before adding anything new to your space, ask, "Does this serve me or just fill silence?"

Curating means surrounding yourself only with what adds meaning, utility, or joy.

Decoration without intention often leads to debt and dust.

3. Align the Flow

Rearrange your space so it supports your actual lifestyle, not an aspirational one.

If your treadmill has become a coat rack, let it go. If your dining room table only gathers mail, reclaim it for connection. A space designed for living invites gratitude — and gratitude reduces the urge to acquire.

Real-Life Story:

The Downsized Dream

When my clients Rebecca and John decided to sell their 3,800-square-foot home, their friends thought they'd lost their minds. They had "made it" — the vaulted ceilings, the home theater, the gourmet kitchen. But with each passing year, the mortgage felt heavier, the upkeep endless. The very house that was supposed to symbolize success had become a source of stress.

Even their golden retriever, Tucker, seemed to feel it — pacing from room to room, restless and overstimulated, never quite sure where to rest. During one of our dog training sessions, I noticed how his behavior mirrored the energy of their home: too much space, too many distractions, and no clear boundaries. The house looked perfect, but it didn't feel peaceful — and Tucker wasn't the only one who sensed that.

After months of hesitation, they sold it all and moved into a bright, two-bedroom cottage on the edge of town. For the first time in years, they could breathe. Their weekends weren't consumed by lawn care and repair calls. They traveled, cooked simple meals together, and found themselves laughing again over dinner instead of calculating bills.

Rebecca once told me, "I thought I'd miss the space. But what I really missed all those years was us."

Downsizing didn't shrink their life — it expanded it.

Rebecca and John's experience is a reminder that a home isn't defined by its size — it's defined by how it feels to live there. When your space starts to drain more energy than it gives, it's a signal something's off-balance.

Rosemarie Williams

Spend a quiet moment simply observing your surroundings. Notice where tension gathers and where ease naturally returns. The places that leave you feeling unsettled often reveal more about emotional or financial clutter than any budget ever could.

Reflection:

Walking Through Your Space with New Eyes

Take a quiet moment to walk through your home as if you were visiting it for the first time. Don't straighten, tidy, or judge. Just observe.

- What emotions surface in each room?
- What stories are your possessions telling about your priorities?
- Which spaces feel peaceful, and which feel like pressure?
- If your home were a financial statement, where would it show overspending, neglect, or investment?

Write down your observations. These aren't about shame; they're about awareness.

When you learn to "read" your home, you gain insight into your financial behaviors without opening a single spreadsheet.

Action Step: The Room Reset

Choose one room this week and commit to a simple *reset*. You're not redesigning — you're realigning.

1. Clear every surface and shelf.
2. Put back only what serves a clear purpose or sparks calm.
3. Notice how the space feels when it's not performing.

Then, observe your spending habits over the next few days. When your environment feels settled, your brain stops searching for comfort through consumption. That's how peace begins — quietly, in the space between needing and having.

Closing Thought

Your home is the clearest reflection of your inner and financial world.

When it feels peaceful, you spend with clarity.

When it feels chaotic, you reach for escape — often through the very habits that create more chaos.

The good news is, you can rewrite that pattern — one drawer, one decision, one intentional moment at a time.

Financial freedom doesn't always start in the bank. Sometimes, it starts in the living room.

CHAPTER 5

The Emotional Price Tag

Chapter 5

Every item you keep carries a story and a cost

The Hidden Weight Behind What We Keep

It's not always about money. What we hold onto often costs something far more personal — a corner of space, a bit of energy, or a piece of our peace. Over time, those small costs add up to a life that feels heavy when it should feel light.

When you look around your home, you might see furniture, boxes, or décor. But if you look closer, you'll also see stories — the wedding gift you never used, the clothes from a version of yourself you no longer are, the heirlooms you didn't choose but feel obligated to keep.

Every object is a thread tied to memory, meaning, or identity. And some of those threads quietly pull you backward.

We keep things because they once mattered. We keep them because letting go feels like betrayal — of a person, a dream, or a past self. But when the past begins to crowd out the present, you start paying emotional rent for things that no longer serve you.

Downsizing, at its core, isn't about throwing things away. It's about recognizing what your possessions are costing you emotionally and reclaiming that energy for what's next.

The Guilt Loop

Guilt is one of the strongest forces keeping clutter in place. It's subtle, persuasive, and almost always disguised as obligation.

You might hear it whispering things like:

- "It was a gift — I can't get rid of it."
- "It was expensive — I should use it."
- "It's still good — someone could use it."
- "I'll regret it if I let it go."

But guilt doesn't preserve meaning — it preserves stagnation. You're not dishonoring the person who gave you something by releasing it. You're honoring the space they once held in your life and acknowledging that their presence mattered more than the object ever did.

The truth is, when someone gives you a gift, the act of giving is complete. The purpose of that item was fulfilled the moment gratitude was exchanged. Everything after that is optional.

Letting go of a gift doesn't mean rejecting love; it means keeping your home open to the next chapter of it.

When "Sentimental" Becomes Stuck

Sentiment is beautiful — it connects us to our history. But when sentiment turns into *storage*, it can block us from living the story we're in now.

Maybe you're holding onto:

- Boxes of old family items you never open.
- Clothes from the "best years" that no longer fit your body or your life.

- Collections that were once hobbies but now just collect dust.

Every one of these things holds emotional weight — nostalgia, regret, or hope. And while these feelings are human, they can also keep us tethered to times we've already outgrown.

Here's a truth few people talk about: *letting go of something doesn't erase the memory.* The meaning doesn't live in the object — it lives in you.

Letting Go Without Losing Meaning

Downsizing doesn't mean detaching from your story. It means choosing which chapters you want to display.

Try this approach: **Honor, Release, Redefine.**

1. **Honor it.** Acknowledge what the item represents. Say it out loud. "This quilt reminds me of my grandmother's kindness."

2. **Release it.** Decide that you don't need to physically hold it to emotionally carry it forward.

3. **Redefine it.** Take a photo, write the story behind it, or repurpose part of it into something you'll actually use.

This way, the emotion remains, but the burden doesn't.

For some, creating a "memory box" helps — one small space where meaningful items are kept intentionally, not emotionally. When the box is full, it's time to reevaluate. If everything's meaningful, nothing truly is.

The Fear of Waste

Many people hold onto things because they equate letting go with waste. "What if I need it later?" "It's still good!" "I don't want to be wasteful."

But here's another way to look at it:

Keeping something you never use is its own form of waste — a waste of space, of peace, and of opportunity.

Clutter prevents the things you *do* value from standing out. It traps abundance in a closed loop. The moment you release what you no longer need, you invite circulation — and circulation is the heartbeat of prosperity.

Letting go is not waste. It's redistribution.

You're allowing an item to serve someone else instead of suffocating under the weight of your guilt.

The Emotional Cost of "Someday"

"Someday" is one of the most expensive words in the English language.

Someday I'll use that.
Someday I'll get back into that hobby.
Someday I'll wear that again.

But "someday" rarely comes. And until it does, those items hold your future hostage. They crowd out your present with what-ifs and unfinished intentions.

Ask yourself:

- Is this something I *might* need, or something I *want* to believe I'll use?
- Am I keeping it out of potential or out of fear?

When you let go of "someday," you reclaim today.

From Possession to Presence

The paradox of downsizing is that the less you have, the more present you become.

You start noticing the details again — the light through the window, the rhythm of your mornings, the calm that follows simplicity.

You stop defining your days by what you own and start defining them by what you experience.

This isn't minimalism for its own sake — it's mindfulness. It's trading the weight of "things" for the richness of awareness.

Presence is the ultimate luxury — and unlike stuff, it doesn't depreciate.

Reflection: Questions for Emotional Clarity

- What item in my home carries the most emotional weight — and why?
- What story have I attached to this item that might no longer be true?
- If I let it go, what emotion am I afraid to feel?
- How might I honor the memory without holding onto the material?

- What would my space look like if it reflected who I am *now* — not who I was?

Writing down your answers brings unconscious attachments into conscious awareness. Once they're visible, they start to loosen their grip.

Action Step: The Guilt-Free Let-Go

Choose three items that you've kept out of obligation or guilt. For each one:

1. Write down what emotion it represents.
2. Thank it for what it gave you — a lesson, a memory, a reminder.
3. Donate, repurpose, or responsibly discard it.

Notice how you feel afterward — lighter, freer, maybe even braver. That's the real reward of releasing the emotional price tag.

Closing Thought

Everything in your home either supports your peace or steals it.

Each item asks for your attention, your energy, and your space — even when you're not looking at it.

When you begin to let go of what weighs you down, you're not losing anything. You're *returning* to yourself.

Freedom doesn't come from stripping life bare — it comes from surrounding yourself only with what mirrors your truth.

CHAPTER 6
Debt Detox

Chapter 6

Clearing financial clutter to make room to breathe- freedom

The Silent Weight We Carry

Debt is sneaky.

It doesn't sit on your counter like clutter or stare at you from a closet. It hums quietly in the background — a constant mental load you get used to carrying. You don't always notice it, but it shapes every decision you make.

You might recognize the feeling: that subtle tightening in your chest when a bill arrives, or the avoidance when you glance at your bank app. Debt doesn't just take money — it takes mental bandwidth. It's like having a subscription to stress you can't seem to cancel.

But here's the truth: you don't have to live under it. Debt is not a moral failure or a permanent label. It's a *season*. And just like any other, it can end — with clarity, courage, and consistency.

This chapter isn't about shame; it's about detox. Clearing out what no longer serves you financially so you can breathe again.

Identifying Financial Clutter

If physical clutter fills your home, financial clutter fills your mind. It's the small, unnoticed leaks that drain your resources over time.

Start here:

- Subscriptions you forgot about or barely use.
- Memberships you signed up for "temporarily."
- Duplicate insurances or streaming services.
- Interest payments on credit cards carrying balances longer than you intended.
- Storage fees for items you no longer even remember.

These are the quiet culprits of modern debt — invisible, normalized, and easy to ignore.

The first step of your **Debt Detox** is awareness: seeing where your money is trickling away without purpose.

The Illusion of "Small Payments"

Marketing has trained us to love the word *monthly*.

"Only $29 a month!" sounds harmless. But a $29 commitment made ten times becomes $290. Add in interest, and that harmless number becomes a chain.

Small payments are the emotional equivalent of cluttered counters — each one seems minor, but together they create chaos. You don't feel the weight until the sum starts choking your freedom.

Ask yourself:

- Which payments make my life better?
- Which ones make it *busier*?
- What would I gain emotionally if I cut even one of them?

Freedom starts with subtraction.

The Emotional Side of Debt

Debt is rarely just about math. It's emotional.

We often borrow not because we're careless, but because we're compensating — for lack, fear, or exhaustion.

Sometimes it's survival. Other times, it's the emotional high of "fixing" something temporarily.

But no matter the cause, unexamined debt becomes a mirror of unspoken needs.

Here's what many people discover when they start their Debt Detox:

- Overspending often masks fatigue or self-doubt.
- Avoiding bills often signals shame or overwhelm.
- Justifying payments often hides fear of changing habits.

The goal here isn't guilt. It's recognition.

When you understand what emotion drives your spending, you finally gain control over it.

Reframing Debt: From Burden to Blueprint

Here's the reframe that changes everything: debt isn't just a record of your past choices — it's a *blueprint for your future boundaries*.

Each balance tells a story about how you valued time, comfort, or control. Learning from it doesn't mean reliving it. It means using that awareness to design a life that doesn't require rescue.

Instead of seeing debt as punishment, see it as data — feedback from a system that needs a redesign.

Once you know where the leaks are, you can rebuild stronger.

The Debt–Desire Loop

Debt and desire often dance together. We want something — relief, validation, excitement — and in chasing it, we create another layer of debt that eventually fuels more desire.

It looks like this:

1. Feel discomfort.
2. Spend to feel better.
3. Experience temporary relief.

4. Regret the decision.

5. Seek another purchase to offset the regret.

And so the loop continues — until you decide to interrupt it with awareness.

Breaking the loop doesn't mean giving up joy. It means finding joy that doesn't cost interest.

Your Freedom Formula Reset

Debt Detox is less about deprivation and more about direction. You're not cutting to punish yourself — you're clearing space to breathe. Follow this simple framework: **Track, Cut, Redirect.**

1. **Track**
    - Print or download your last 60 days of statements.
    - Highlight every recurring expense.
    - Categorize each one as *Essential, Optional,* or *Emotional.*

Essentials sustain life. Optionals add convenience. Emotionals are the ones tied to comfort, guilt, or impulse.

2. **Cut**
    - Eliminate one Optional and one Emotional expense this week.
    - Cancel, pause, or renegotiate. Small actions compound quickly.

The money you save isn't just numbers — it's self-trust returning.

3. **Redirect**
    - Redirect what you saved toward your highest-value goal: paying off debt, building an emergency fund, or creating a "Freedom Fund."
    - Watch how quickly progress builds when your money starts reflecting your purpose.

When you redirect your money, you redirect your power.

Simplifying Debt Without Overwhelm

You don't need a complicated system to regain control. Start with clarity, then build consistency.

1. **List every debt** you owe, with balance, minimum payment, and interest rate.

2. **Rank them by payoff priority.** Some prefer to pay smallest first (for motivation). Others target highest interest first (for efficiency). Either is fine — the best plan is the one you'll stick to.

3. **Automate payments** whenever possible to avoid missed fees.

4. **Celebrate every milestone.** Even paying one card off deserves acknowledgment.

Debt reduction isn't just financial — it's emotional liberation in real time.

The Energy Drain You Don't See

Carrying debt is like leaving tabs open on your mental browser. You might not notice them, but they slow everything down. Every time you think about your finances — even subconsciously — a portion of your energy diverts there.

Imagine what would happen if that energy were freed:

- More creativity for projects that fulfill you.
- More patience in your relationships.
- More clarity when making decisions.

Debt Detox is really *life detox*. You're not just balancing accounts — you're restoring your attention to the present moment.

Reflection: Questions to Reclaim Financial Peace

- Which debt causes me the most emotional stress — and why?
- What belief about money keeps me stuck in the same financial pattern?
- What would "financial calm" look like in my everyday life?
- How might I reward myself without spending?

Writing these out helps reframe debt from a hidden shadow into a solvable system. Awareness always precedes action.

Action Step: The "No-Guilt Cancel List"

Take ten minutes today to identify three recurring charges or habits that no longer serve you.

- Cancel at least one immediately.
- Redirect that money to your Freedom Fund.
- Write down how it feels — not what you saved, but what you reclaimed.

Repeat this weekly. One cancellation at a time, you'll begin to feel lighter — not because of what you removed, but because of the control you regained.

Closing Thought

Debt doesn't define you — it reminds you

It reminds you that somewhere along the line, you valued survival or comfort over sustainability. And that's human. But now, you get to choose differently.

When you replace guilt with awareness, every payment becomes progress.

Every canceled charge becomes clarity.

Every small win becomes a declaration: *I'm taking my life back, one decision at a time.*

Because financial freedom isn't about having more money — it's about having more freedom in how you use it.

CHAPTER 7

THE TRUE DEFINITION OF WEALTH

Chapter 7

It's not what you own. It's what you have the freedom to experience

The Myth of More

We've been told that wealth is about numbers — the size of a paycheck, the balance in a bank account, the square footage of a home. But real wealth isn't measured in digits. It's measured in *distance* — the distance between how much you have and how much you *think* you need.

That gap is what creates peace or pressure.

When the gap is wide, you chase.

When it's narrow, you rest.

True wealth isn't the absence of work — it's the absence of worry. It's the quiet confidence of knowing you have enough, that your time is your own, and that your choices align with your values.

Wealth isn't found in "more." It's found in *enough*.

Redefining Rich

Let's reframe the conversation.

Being "rich" has nothing to do with the label society gives you and everything to do with the feeling your life gives you.

You can have a six-figure income and still live paycheck to paycheck emotionally. You can also live modestly and feel deeply abundant. The difference lies in ownership — not of possessions, but of priorities.

Ask yourself:

- Do my days feel meaningful or mechanical?
- Am I spending in alignment with my joy or my image?
- Do I have the freedom to say no — or does money always decide for me?

Real wealth gives you options, not obligations. It's the ability to choose your pace, your peace, and your presence.

The Enough Equation

In Chapter 1, we explored the Freedom Equation:

Space + Simplicity = Peace × Prosperity.

Now, we build on that foundation with what I call **The Enough Equation:**

Contentment = Clarity + Gratitude − Comparison

When you know what truly matters (clarity) and appreciate what already exists (gratitude), comparison naturally loses its grip.

This isn't passive acceptance; it's active fulfillment. You stop asking, "How much more can I get?" and start asking, "How can I fully live what I already have?"

That mindset shift transforms how you spend, save, and even show up in the world.

Time: The Forgotten Currency

We talk about saving money constantly — but how often do we talk about saving *time*?

Time is the one resource that refuses to replenish. You can earn back lost money, but never lost moments. Yet many people trade their most precious hours for things they don't truly want, just to maintain an image of success.

When you downsize your lifestyle, you automatically upsize your time. You get back the Saturday mornings once spent cleaning, organizing, or worrying about maintenance. You get back the mental energy once spent managing payments or juggling commitments.

Time freedom is wealth in its purest form.

And unlike money, it compounds in joy — not in interest.

Ask yourself:

- What parts of my week feel richest?
- Which activities feel like withdrawals instead of deposits?
- How can I invest my time in what multiplies peace, not pressure?

From Possession to Purpose

There comes a point when accumulating things no longer satisfies — and often, that point arrives quietly.

The excitement of buying fades faster each time. You start craving experiences over objects, memories over milestones.

Purpose becomes the new luxury.

True prosperity isn't about having everything — it's about doing something meaningful with what you already have.

When you align your finances and lifestyle with purpose, wealth stops being an external chase and becomes an internal rhythm.

You no longer spend to feel alive — you live to feel aligned.

When Enough Was Finally Enough

A few years ago, I met a man named Luis, a retired executive who had spent thirty years climbing the ladder. On paper, he had everything: the big house, the cars, the travel photos. But when he retired, he realized something startling — he didn't know who he was without the constant motion.

He sold his house, moved into a small lake cabin, and began volunteering at a local animal shelter twice a week. One day he told me, "For the first time in my life, I'm not chasing Fridays. Every day feels like Saturday."

Luis didn't give up wealth. He redefined it. And in that redefinition, he found freedom.

Gratitude as a Financial Strategy

Gratitude might sound sentimental, but it's one of the most powerful financial tools you have. When you practice gratitude consistently, it shifts your mindset from *lack* to *abundance.*

People who live in gratitude spend differently.

They buy less impulsively.

They appreciate experiences more deeply. They focus on maintenance instead of replacement.

Try this simple exercise:

For one week, before you make a purchase — any purchase — write down three things you already have that serve a similar purpose. Notice how it changes your desire to buy. Gratitude is the pause that transforms impulse into intention.

Wealth grows in the space between wanting and waiting.

Financial Peace: The Ultimate Status Symbol

Financial peace doesn't always mean financial perfection. It's not about having zero debt, multiple streams of income, or a fancy retirement plan.

It's about waking up without the constant buzz of anxiety around money. It's about knowing that your lifestyle fits comfortably within your reality — and still leaves room for joy.

That kind of peace is magnetic. It radiates confidence and self-trust. It inspires others far more than luxury ever could.

Because at the end of the day, peace is the only thing you can't buy — you can only build it.

Reflection: Redefining What "Rich" Means to You

- What does a wealthy life look like for *you* — not society, not family, not social media?
- Which areas of your life already feel abundant?
- Where are you still measuring yourself by someone else's scale?
- What would "enough" feel like if you decided it today?

Write down your answers without censoring them. Let them surprise you.

Often, true wealth reveals itself not in what you add, but in what you finally stop chasing.

Action Step: The Contentment Inventory

This week, take a "Contentment Inventory."

1. List five things you already have that make daily life easier or richer.
2. List three experiences from the last year that brought you joy but cost little or nothing.
3. Review your spending for the month — highlight anything that didn't add genuine happiness or growth.

Then ask yourself:

If I redirected even 10% of my spending from things to meaning, how would my life expand?

The goal isn't guilt — it's gratitude. To recognize that real wealth was never out there waiting. It's been living quietly inside your choices all along.

Closing Thought

The moment you stop defining wealth by what's visible, you start living richly in ways that matter.

You stop performing success and start *experiencing* it.

Real wealth isn't louder, bigger, or flashier. It's quieter.

It's the laughter that doesn't need an audience.

The time you no longer trade for approval.

The deep exhale that says, "This is enough."

Because when your life fits, it doesn't have to prove anything — it simply shines.

CHAPTER 8
Designing a Life That Fits

Chapter 8

You can't live your best life in someone else's blueprint

The Myth of the "Ideal Life"

We spend so much of our lives trying to fit into molds that were never made for us.

We chase careers because they look good on paper.

We decorate homes because they look good in magazines.

We fill calendars because we think full equals valuable.

Somewhere along the way, we stopped designing *our* lives — and started inheriting everyone else's.

The truth? There's no universal version of success. There's only *alignment* — a life that fits who you really are and what truly matters to you.

Designing a life that fits isn't about shrinking your dreams. It's about tailoring them — so your outer world finally matches your inner values.

Step One: Clarify What "Fit" Means to You

Before you can design a life that fits, you need to define what that even looks like.

For some, it means peace. For others, mobility. For many, it's freedom from financial or emotional pressure.

Here's a simple truth: fit isn't about *perfection*. It's about *function*.

Does your life function in a way that supports your health, your growth, and your happiness?

Ask yourself:

- What do I want my days to feel like?
- What do I want less of — and what do I want more of?
- If I stopped performing, what would I naturally gravitate toward?

Write your answers without trying to impress anyone. Clarity doesn't come from logic — it comes from honesty.

The "Life That Fits" Framework

There are three pillars to designing a life that fits: **Clarity, Consistency, and Contentment.**

1. Clarity: Know What Matters

This pillar is about awareness — seeing your true priorities without the noise of obligation or comparison.

You can't build balance around what you *think* you should want. You can only build around what genuinely lights you up.

Clarity comes from stillness.

Take time regularly to step away from screens, noise, and external opinions.

The quieter you become, the clearer you hear yourself.

2. Consistency: Live What You Value

Once you know what matters, consistency turns awareness into action.

This means your daily choices, not your occasional goals, shape your reality.

Ask:

- Does my spending reflect my priorities?
- Does my schedule reflect what I say I value most?
- Do my surroundings reflect calm or chaos?

Design is revealed in patterns — not in big events, but in small habits repeated daily.

3. Contentment: Protect Your Peace

Contentment doesn't mean settling. It means not letting the constant pull for more rob you of what's already good. It's the discipline of satisfaction — the art of saying, *"I have enough for now, and I'm still growing."*

When clarity and consistency meet contentment, your life stops competing — and starts harmonizing.

From Busyness to Balance

We glorify being busy as if exhaustion were a badge of honor. But busyness is not productivity. It's distraction in disguise.

If you're always racing, you can't design. Design requires pause — deliberate thought about how your energy flows through your days.

Ask yourself:

- What am I doing out of genuine purpose versus obligation?
- What am I maintaining simply because it exists?
- What could I remove today that would instantly make my life feel lighter?

When you downsize your commitments with the same care you downsize your possessions, you start living intentionally instead of reactively.

Rebuilding Routine Around What Matters

The structure of your day either drains or sustains you. One of the simplest ways to align your life is to design your routine — not around efficiency, but around energy.

Here's a framework to try:

1. **Morning Grounding** – Start the day with awareness instead of input. A few moments of stillness, reflection, or gratitude can reset your focus before the world's noise takes over.

2. **Midday Check-In** – Pause halfway through your day to ask, "Am I still in alignment with what matters?" A two-minute reset can prevent a two-week spiral.

3. **Evening Release** – End the day with closure. Write down what went well, what needs adjusting, and one thing you're grateful for. Let that be enough.

Your calendar should feel like a reflection of your peace — not a battlefield for your worth.

Mini Design Exercise: The 3-Column Life Audit

Grab a notebook and draw three columns labeled: **Keep**, **Change**, and **Let Go.**

Under **Keep**, list what's working — the routines, habits, and relationships that add value and peace.

Under **Change**, list what needs adjustment — what could improve with intention.

Under **Let Go**, list what no longer serves you — commitments, spaces, or identities that feel outdated.

This simple exercise is deceptively powerful. It takes the abstract idea of "design" and turns it into visible, actionable clarity.

Redesigning Your Environment

Your surroundings either support or sabotage your efforts to stay aligned.

Now that you've learned how to simplify and declutter, use your space as a tool to reinforce your vision.

Ask:

- Does my home make me feel calm or overwhelmed?
- Are my favorite spaces functional or just "decorated"?

- Do I feel inspired where I work, eat, and rest?

A life that fits has an environment that feels like an extension of your inner peace, not a distraction from it.

Even small shifts — a clear counter, a rearranged workspace, a room used for its real purpose — can change how you experience your days.

The "One Week Fit Test"

For the next seven days, live as if your new, simplified, values-aligned lifestyle is already in place.

Eat, spend, rest, and schedule in harmony with the life you're designing — not the one you're trying to escape.

Pay attention to:

- What feels natural and energizing.
- What feels forced or unnecessary.
- Which boundaries you honored and which you let slip.

At the end of the week, review your experience. This isn't about perfection — it's a prototype.

Design isn't a one-time act; it's a process of refinement.

Reflection: Designing on Your Terms

- What would my ideal "day in alignment" look like?
- Which activities drain my energy the fastest?
- What boundaries would I need to set to protect my peace?
- What small changes could make my life feel like mine again?

Write your answers down, not as goals but as design notes. You're not chasing a different life — you're shaping the one you already have.

Action Step: Reclaim One Space, One Habit, One Expense

Pick one of each category this week:

- **Space:** Simplify one physical area.
- **Habit:** Replace one draining routine with one uplifting action.
- **Expense:** Eliminate one unnecessary payment and redirect the savings toward your "Freedom Fund."

This three-part realignment builds momentum. Every small change becomes proof that your life can fit better — not someday, but right now.

Closing Thought

Designing a life that fits isn't about starting over. It's about returning home — to your own rhythm, your own priorities, your own version of peace.

The world will always tell you to want more. But true power comes from choosing *better* instead.

Because when your life fits, you stop striving to keep up — and start living to keep whole.

CHAPTER 9

The Ripple Effect of Less

Chapter 9

How simplifying changes relationships, productivity, and self-worth

The Unexpected Side Effect of Simplicity

When you first begin downsizing, it feels practical — a way to free space, save money, or reduce chaos. But at some point, something deeper happens.

You start to feel lighter — not just in your home, but in your conversations, your decisions, your very sense of self.

This is the ripple effect.

It's what happens when you stop measuring your life by what you accumulate and start measuring it by what you *experience*.

The truth is, simplifying doesn't just change your space. It changes how you show up in the world.

Less Stuff, More Self

When the noise of clutter quiets down, your inner voice gets louder. You start noticing what you actually like, not what you thought you were supposed to like.

Simplicity gives you back *you*.

It's astonishing how much of our identity gets tangled up in our possessions and routines.

The designer bag that once represented confidence now feels irrelevant.
The constant social calendar that once felt validating now feels exhausting.

With less to manage, you become more aware of who you are — not the version shaped by marketing or comparison, but the real one that's been there all along.

You begin to choose not out of impulse, but intention. And that single shift — from reacting to choosing — is the heartbeat of self-trust.

Ask yourself:

- What feels most "me" when everything else gets quiet?
- What would I do differently if I stopped proving and started living?

The answers reveal more than any self-help book ever could.

Once the external noise fades and the distractions fall away, you start to notice something deeper — the quiet truth of who you've always been.

Simplicity has a way of turning down the volume on everything that isn't you.

And in that stillness, your real preferences, values, and rhythms begin to rise to the surface.

This is the part of the journey where clarity meets self-awareness. You're not just organizing your environment; you're remembering yourself.

The exercise below will help you identify what feels most authentic — what feels most *you* — when everything else gets quiet.

Mini-Exercise: Finding Your True Fit Zone

When everything around you slows down — no notifications, no noise, no obligations — who are you then? That's your *True Fit Zone*: the place where your energy, peace, and authenticity naturally meet.

This exercise helps you uncover it.

Step 1: Create Quiet

Set aside 10–15 minutes. Turn off your phone, lower the lights, and sit somewhere comfortable.

You're not meditating — just letting your thoughts settle like dust in still air.

Step 2: Revisit Your Moments of Ease

Think back to the last time you felt calm, content, and unhurried. Ask yourself:

- Where was I?

- What was I doing (or not doing)?
- Who was with me — or was I alone?
- What emotions were present?

Write freely for a few minutes. Don't edit; let memory guide you.

Step 3: Identify Common Threads

Now look for patterns.

- Do your calm moments involve nature, creativity, animals, quiet, or movement?
- Are they usually solitary or social?
- Do they happen at home, outside, or during simple tasks?

These clues reveal the *conditions* under which your truest self thrives.

Step 4: Define Your "Feels Like Me" Statement

Complete this sentence:

"When everything else gets quiet, what feels most *me* is _____."

You might write:

"When everything else gets quiet, what feels most me is walking my dog at sunrise — no agenda, no performance, just rhythm and breath." Or "What feels most me is writing late at night when the world's asleep and my thoughts have room to stretch."

Keep it short and honest. One or two lines is enough.

Step 5: Protect It

Now — circle one small way to make more space for that feeling in your daily life.

You're not scheduling a new routine. You're prioritizing *alignment*. Maybe it's ten quiet minutes in the morning, an evening walk, or saying no to one unnecessary commitment each week.

This is where less starts expanding your life — not by doing more, but by doing what fits.

Closing Reflection:

Your *True Fit Zone* is your personal compass.

Whenever life starts feeling crowded, come back to this question:

"What feels most me when everything else gets quiet?"

The answer will change with each season — but the peace you find in listening to it never will.

How Simplicity Strengthens Relationships

When your life is cluttered — physically or mentally — connection takes a back seat. You're too distracted to listen fully, too rushed to engage deeply.

But when you simplify, you create space not just in your home, but in your relationships.

Presence becomes your new love language.

You start spending real time with people instead of multitasking through moments. Conversations go deeper because your mind isn't juggling mental to-do lists.

You notice things — tone, expression, the pause before someone says something hard.

You also start choosing relationships more consciously.

As your space becomes intentional, your circle often follows suit. You no longer have energy for people who drain, manipulate, or compete. And that's not selfish — it's stewardship.

Healthy connection thrives in uncluttered spaces — where honesty replaces performance, and time spent together feels like a gift, not an obligation.

Reflection prompt:

- Who in my life feels like peace, and who feels like pressure?
- What boundaries would help me protect the relationships that matter most?

From Chaos to Clarity in Work and Creativity

Less clutter means fewer distractions, and fewer distractions mean greater focus.

It's not just about a tidy desk — it's about a clear mind.

When you remove excess, your creativity expands.

You start finishing projects you used to procrastinate. You think more clearly, decide faster, and waste less energy second-guessing yourself.

Simplicity restores mental bandwidth. It makes space for ideas to breathe.

If you're someone who's been spinning in "always busy" mode, downsizing your commitments can actually *increase* your output — because your energy is no longer scattered. It's concentrated.

Try this:

For one week, choose one priority per day. Not five, not three — one.
Notice how much more satisfying your days feel when you give your full attention to what truly matters.

Redefining Worth

In a world that equates worth with productivity and possessions, choosing less can feel like rebellion. But it's a rebellion worth leading.

When you begin to value calm over constant motion, you discover that your worth was never tied to your output — it was tied to your existence.

That's the real ripple:

When you no longer need to *earn* your value, you stop chasing validation through things, achievements, or attention. You show up grounded, self-directed, and at peace.

And people feel that

Your confidence stops shouting and starts radiating.

When Simplicity Inspires Others

Here's something beautiful: you won't even have to convince anyone to change. When you live lighter, people notice. They see it in the way you move through life — unhurried, uncluttered, unbothered.

They see it in how your home feels calm, how your conversations have depth, how your decisions are rooted in peace instead of pressure.

That's how movements begin — not with slogans, but with quiet example.

When you choose less, you become a mirror that shows others what's possible.

And that's the real influence — not perfection, but presence.

Freedom to Dream Again

When your days aren't filled with managing the excess, you finally have space to dream again.

Maybe you rediscover a hobby you'd buried under obligations. Maybe you plan that trip you've postponed for years. Maybe you simply sit still and feel a kind of joy you can't buy.

Simplicity gives birth to curiosity. And curiosity leads to possibility.

Downsizing your life isn't just about removing clutter — it's about reclaiming *potential*.

When you clear the noise, the whispers of purpose get louder.

Ask yourself:

- What dreams have I postponed because I was too busy maintaining?
- What could I create with the time, energy, and peace I now have?

Those aren't idle questions — they're invitations to begin again.

Reflection: Recognizing Your Ripple

Pause for a moment and consider the effects of your own transformation.

- How has simplifying changed the way you communicate, spend, or create?
- What ripple have others noticed — even if they haven't said it?
- What kind of influence do you want your calm to have in the world around you?

Write these reflections down.

This is how you anchor gratitude and momentum — by seeing your progress as a wave still expanding.

Action Step: The Freedom Vision Board

Create a vision board — not of *things,* but of *feelings and experiences.* Include images, words, or quotes that represent freedom, peace, and presence.

Examples: a sunrise for calm mornings, a dinner table with friends for connection, a mountain path for balance, a blank notebook for creative space.

Hang it where you'll see it daily.

Let it remind you that you didn't simplify to have less — you simplified to *feel more.*

Closing Thought

The ripple effect of less is quiet but undeniable.

You think you're simplifying your space — but you're really strengthening your soul.

You spend less, yet you give more.

You own less, yet you live fuller.

You control less, yet you experience more freedom.

Because peace, once chosen, multiplies.

And the moment you decide to live lighter, the world around you begins to rise to meet that energy.

CHAPTER 10
SUSTAINING FREEDOM

Chapter 10

Keeping simplicity alive in a world that sells complexity

Freedom Isn't a Finish Line

By the time you reach this point in your downsizing journey, life already feels lighter. You've let go of clutter, redefined what matters, and designed a life that finally fits.

But freedom, like health or happiness, isn't something you achieve once — it's something you maintain.

The real challenge begins after the excitement fades.

When the house is clear, the budget balanced, and the noise gone, life doesn't stop testing your resolve. The world keeps whispering: *"Buy more." "Do more." "Be more."*

Sustaining freedom means learning how to protect your peace in a culture addicted to chaos. It's about becoming the calm in your own storm — not through perfection, but through rhythm.

The Maintenance Mindset

Freedom doesn't require constant effort — it requires consistent awareness.

Think of it like tending a garden: you don't have to replant everything each season, but you do have to pull the weeds before they take over again.

A *maintenance mindset* keeps your life clear without falling back into old patterns. It's less about control and more about conscious upkeep — a natural rhythm of evaluating, editing, and realigning as life evolves.

Ask yourself:

- What habits keep my days balanced and clear?
- Which areas of my life start to slip when I stop paying attention?
- How can I check in with myself before the clutter — mental, emotional, or financial — starts creeping back in?

When you treat awareness as an act of care instead of correction, you turn maintenance into mindfulness.

Creating Your Freedom Routine

Freedom is sustained by simple, repeatable actions. You don't need a complicated system — just a few anchor habits that keep your clarity intact.

Try starting with these:

Daily:

- Take five minutes to reset one space — a counter, your desk, your inbox.
- Review your energy, not your productivity: *Did I live in alignment today?*
- Express one moment of gratitude, no matter how small.

Weekly:

- Review your schedule. Eliminate one task that no longer fits.
- Track one spending habit that could use refining.
- Plan one intentional moment of joy — something to look forward to.

Monthly:

- Revisit your budget and simplify where you can.
- Evaluate your commitments: is everything on your calendar still essential or meaningful?
- Reflect on your Freedom Equation:

Space + Simplicity = Peace × Prosperity

Where is it thriving, and where is it slipping?

Consistency here matters more than intensity. The small, repeated acts of alignment are what keep you from drifting back into overwhelm.

The Seasonal Life Audit

Every few months, life changes shape — your priorities shift, your routines evolve, and your needs adjust. That's why freedom must be flexible.

A *Seasonal Life Audit* helps you realign your environment, finances, and focus with your current season — not the one you were living six months ago.

Here's how to do it:

1. **Reflect.**
   Ask, *What's working? What's not? What needs to be released or refreshed?*

2. **Reassess.**
   Walk through your spaces. Notice where clutter is sneaking back in. Check your spending and subscriptions for leaks. Look at your time — what's overbooked or undernourished?

3. **Realign.**
   Adjust your habits, space, and goals to match the person you're becoming, not the one you used to be.

4. **Recommit.**
   Write down your new focus for the season — a simple phrase or intention like "protect my peace," "work with purpose," or "slow down and savor."

When you make realignment a ritual, change stops feeling like failure — it starts feeling like growth.

Guarding Your Boundaries

Freedom fades quickly when boundaries blur.

One "yes" out of guilt, one "just this once" purchase, one skipped rest day — that's how clutter begins its quiet return.

Boundaries aren't walls; they're filters. They decide what gets your energy and what doesn't.

A few boundary reminders worth revisiting often:

- You don't owe anyone access to your time simply because they ask.

- You're allowed to pause before committing — or to say no without explanation.

- You can value peace over pleasing.

Protecting your boundaries is protecting your clarity. The more peaceful your inner world, the easier it is to sustain an uncluttered outer one.

The Three-Box Rule for Life

This simple principle keeps your environment and habits from overcrowding again.

Label three imaginary boxes in your mind:

Keep, Release, Replace.

Whenever you feel life getting full again — whether it's your home, your commitments, or your calendar — pause and ask:

- **Keep:** What still adds value, joy, or necessity?
- **Release:** What no longer serves the person I'm becoming?
- **Replace:** What new habit, mindset, or boundary will strengthen my peace?

You can use this same approach for nearly everything — from decluttering your closet to refining relationships or simplifying work routines.

Freedom isn't about freezing your life in minimalism; it's about keeping it *mobile* — able to breathe, evolve, and expand in ways that still feel aligned.

How to Handle "Freedom Fatigue"

Even the most mindful person can hit a wall. Maybe you get busy again, maybe a crisis arises, or maybe you just forget how good it felt to live light.

That's normal.

The key is to recognize the symptoms of "freedom fatigue" early — the subtle signs you're slipping back into old patterns:

- You're buying things to celebrate or comfort yourself.
- Your schedule is filling faster than your energy can sustain.
- You're feeling anxious, scattered, or short-tempered for no clear reason.

When this happens, don't scold yourself — reset gently. Take one small, symbolic action to reclaim your peace. Clean a drawer. Cancel a meeting. Take a walk without your phone. The goal isn't to rebuild all at once — it's to remind yourself what freedom feels like.

Reflection: Your Ongoing Commitment to Peace

Take a few minutes to write freely on these questions:

- How does freedom feel in my daily life right now?
- What area of my life most needs a "reset"?
- What boundaries or habits have helped me stay centered?
- What one thing could I recommit to this month to protect my peace?

These reflections turn awareness into accountability — not through pressure, but through presence.

Action Step: The Freedom Maintenance Plan

This plan helps keep your freedom intentional and visible. Write it down or print it where you can see it often.

My Freedom Maintenance Plan

Every Morning:

I begin the day grounded and grateful. I check in with myself before checking in with the world.

Every Week:

I eliminate one thing — physical, digital, or emotional — that no longer fits.

Every Month:

I realign my spending, space, and schedule to reflect what matters most.

Every Season:

I celebrate progress, refresh priorities, and make room for what's next.

Freedom isn't something I hold — it's something I live, one conscious choice at a time.

Closing Thought

Freedom, at its core, is stewardship — the ongoing care of what matters most.

It's not about rigid systems or endless restraint. It's about staying awake to your own life.

The longer you live with less, the more you realize that simplicity isn't the absence of abundance.

It's the awareness that abundance was never about more — it was about *enough*.

And when you protect that awareness, you don't just sustain freedom.

You become it.

CONCLUSION

Freedom Is the New Rich

Conclusion

The Moment You Realize You Have Enough

There's a moment — quiet, almost unremarkable — when you realize you no longer crave "more."

You look around your life and feel a deep, unexpected calm. You've traded noise for space, pressure for presence, and constant pursuit for steady peace.

That moment isn't flashy or dramatic.

It's something simpler — the sound of your own breathing without hurry, the stillness of a room that finally feels like yours, the ease of knowing you've stopped competing with ghosts.

That's what wealth feels like now. Not the rush of acquisition, but the relief of enough.

The Journey You've Taken

You started this journey thinking it was about space — the drawers, the closets, the square footage. But somewhere along the way, you discovered it was never really about stuff.

It was about *self*.

Each room you cleared mirrored a corner of your mind. Each decision to let go mirrored an act of courage. Each new boundary mirrored a declaration: *My life will no longer be defined by excess — but by ease.*

You downsized the noise and upsized your awareness. You learned that financial freedom doesn't begin with earning more — it begins with wanting less.

And along the way, you found something far greater than balance. You found clarity.

The New Definition of Rich

For generations, we've been told that wealth is measured in accumulation — assets, possessions, influence. But a new kind of wealth is emerging, one that can't be flaunted or financed.

Freedom is the new rich.
It's waking up without dread or debt.
It's being able to spend time instead of just earning it.
It's saying no without guilt and yes without fear.
It's peace that doesn't require performance.

That's the kind of wealth no economy can measure — and no market can take away.

The Power of Living Light

Living light isn't about owning little. It's about carrying only what belongs to you — emotionally, financially, and spiritually.

When you live light, you don't just move through the world differently — the world moves differently around you.

People sense your calm and gravitate toward it.

Your home becomes a place of rest, not storage.

Your time becomes meaningful, not managed.

Your choices become simple, not reactive.

And the beauty is, the more peace you carry, the more abundance you attract — because freedom, once claimed, creates space for everything that matters.

Reflection: Looking Back and Forward

Take a moment to look at how far you've come.

Not just in what you've released, but in who you've grown into.

Ask yourself:

- What does freedom look like for me now?
- What did I once believe I needed to feel secure — and do I still believe it?
- What's the next small way I can live even lighter, freer, truer?

You don't have to have every answer.
You just have to keep asking with intention.

A Final Word

Freedom doesn't announce itself with fanfare. It arrives quietly — in the spaces you've cleared, the debts you've released, the boundaries you've built, and the gratitude you've chosen.

You started with a desire for less.

You ended with a life that feels like *more*.

Because the richest people aren't those with the most possessions — they're the ones who wake up grateful, grounded, and free.

And that's exactly who you've become.

Freedom is the new rich.

And now, it's yours to keep.

Afterword:

From My Heart to Yours

When I first started writing this book, I thought it would be about space — clearing closets, cutting clutter, simplifying finances. But the truth revealed itself along the way: *this book was never about less.* It was always about *freedom.*

The kind of freedom that doesn't come from a single big decision, but from a thousand small ones — the choices we make every day to stop performing and start living.

I didn't always understand that.

There was a time when I thought success was about accumulating — things, titles, achievements. I thought "busy" meant productive, and "more" meant secure. But with every layer I added, I lost a little more of myself.

It took slowing down to finally see that I wasn't missing out — I was simply missing *me.*

That's what downsizing taught me: freedom doesn't come from subtraction alone. It comes from alignment — when your space, your schedule, your spending, and your spirit all work together instead of against each other.

It's not about perfection or minimalism for its own sake. It's about peace — the kind that lets you breathe again.

So if you're here at the end of this book wondering what's next, here's my advice:

Don't rush to fill the space you've created.

Let it breathe. Let it speak.

Give yourself permission to rest in the quiet before you reach for anything new. That quiet — that pause — is where you meet yourself again.

And when you do, you'll realize that what you were chasing all along wasn't more money or more things. It was more *meaning*. And that, my friend, is what freedom really is.

Thank you for taking this journey with me — for trusting me to walk alongside you through the letting go, the rebuilding, and the rediscovering.

I hope this book didn't just teach you how to simplify your life, but how to *live it fully*.

Remember: you don't need to have everything to feel rich. You just need to have *yourself* — grounded, grateful, and free.

Here's to living lighter, loving deeper, and finding joy in the space you've made.

With gratitude and freedom,

Rosemarie

Reader's Reflection & Discussion Guide

A companion to deepen your journey toward a life that fits.

1. Rethinking "More"

- What did "success" used to mean to you — and has that definition changed after reading this book?

- When in your life did "more" stop feeling fulfilling and start feeling heavy?

- Which part of your old lifestyle (physical or emotional) felt most like clutter, and why?

- What surprised you most about how "less" actually made space for *more* of what matters?

2. The Cost of Having It All

- What hidden costs — time, energy, or peace — have you been paying to maintain a lifestyle that no longer fits?

- Which small financial or emotional "leaks" did you recognize in yourself after reading Chapter 1?

- Have you ever confused comfort with freedom? What does true comfort look like now?

- If you had to rewrite your "Freedom Equation" for your own life, what would it be?

3. Decluttering the Inner and Outer Worlds

- What area of your home most reflects how you've been feeling internally?

- How does your physical space affect your financial habits, and vice versa?

- What was the hardest thing for you to let go of — and what emotion was tied to it?

- What does your *ideal* environment feel like now that you've redefined wealth and peace?

4. Redefining Wealth

- What does "enough" mean to you now?

- When you imagine wealth beyond money, what comes to mind first?

- Which "currency" — time, energy, or presence — do you most want to protect moving forward?

- If freedom truly is the new rich, how will you measure prosperity in your daily life?

5. Designing a Life That Fits

- What routines, relationships, or responsibilities feel most aligned with your values today?

- Where are you still trying to fit into someone else's expectations?

- How would your calendar look if it truly reflected your priorities?
- What small design change (in your space, habits, or mindset) could make your days feel lighter?

6. The Ripple Effect of Less

- How has simplifying changed your confidence or self-perception?
- Have others noticed your shift — and how have they responded to it?
- What's one new boundary you've built that's improved your peace or relationships?
- What new possibilities have emerged now that you're living lighter?

7. Sustaining Freedom

- How do you know when clutter — of any kind — is starting to creep back in?
- What practices or rituals help you maintain balance without rigidity?
- What season of life are you in right now, and how might your version of "freedom" evolve next?
- What would it mean to treat simplicity not as a phase, but as a lifelong rhythm?

8. The Heart of the Journey

- What was your most meaningful "aha moment" while reading this book?

- Which story or exercise resonated with you the most — and why?

- If you could share one message from this book with a friend, what would it be?

- How has this journey changed your definition of *home* — inside and out?

Final Reflection: Your Freedom Statement

Take a quiet moment to write your own declaration of freedom — one or two sentences that capture how you want to live from this point forward.

Examples:

"My life fits because I no longer chase more; I choose meaning."
"I measure wealth in peace, time, and connection — not possessions."
"I am free, not because I have less, but because what I have now fits me perfectly."

Write yours below, sign and date it, and revisit it whenever life starts to feel heavy again.

Resources & Recommended Reading
Because freedom doesn't end on the last page.

The journey to simplicity doesn't stop when the book closes — it expands.

The resources that follow are meant to keep your momentum alive: tools, books, and ideas that will help you protect your peace, refine your routines, and stay inspired to live a life that truly fits.

Take what resonates, leave what doesn't, and keep building your version of freedom — one intentional choice at a time.

Practical Tools for Everyday Simplicity

1. The "Freedom Equation" Worksheet

A printable guide (or journal page) you can create for yourself: List one way each week you can create more *space* or *simplicity* — then track the peace and prosperity it brings.

Example columns: *What I released / What I gained / How it felt.*

2. The 10-Minute Declutter

Set a timer for 10 minutes each day. Pick one small area — a drawer, a shelf, an email folder — and clear it completely. Small daily momentum creates big emotional shifts.

3. The "No-Spend Day" Challenge

Choose one day each week to spend nothing. Use that day to enjoy what you already own — cook from your pantry, explore your town, or rest. Notice how it rewires your sense of abundance.

4. The 3-Column Life Audit (Keep / Change / Let Go)

Use this quick reflection every season to stay aligned with your priorities. It's a simple way to prevent clutter — physical or emotional — from creeping back in.

5. The Freedom Fund

Open a small savings account or envelope labeled *Freedom Fund*. Every time you resist an impulse purchase, move that money there instead.

You're not just saving — you're reinforcing choice over chaos.

Recommended Reading: Living Light & Financial Clarity

These titles complement your message of simplicity, intention, and freedom:

Simplifying & Minimalism

- *The More of Less* by Joshua Becker
- *Essentialism: The Disciplined Pursuit of Less* by Greg McKeown
- *Soulful Simplicity* by Courtney Carver
- *Goodbye, Things* by Fumio Sasaki

Money Mindset & Financial Freedom

- *Your Money or Your Life* by Vicki Robin & Joe Dominguez
- *The Psychology of Money* by Morgan Housel
- *I Will Teach You to Be Rich* by Ramit Sethi (for practical budgeting with flexibility)
- *The Total Money Makeover* by Dave Ramsey (for debt reduction fundamentals)

Mindful Living & Presence

- *The Untethered Soul* by Michael A. Singer
- *Atomic Habits* by James Clear
- *The Gifts of Imperfection* by Brené Brown
- *The Joy of Less* by Francine Jay

Digital & Lifestyle Resources

- **Becoming Minimalist (Joshua Becker)** – becomingminimalist.com
Articles and courses on simplifying your home, time, and priorities.

- **Mr. Money Mustache** – mrmoneymustache.com Practical and humorous advice on financial independence and intentional living.

- **The Minimalists Podcast** – theminimalists.com/podcast Insightful discussions on decluttering, purpose, and rethinking success.

- **Zen Habits (Leo Babauta)** – zenhabits.net A long-standing resource for mindfulness, simplicity, and gentle habit change.

Creating Your Own Freedom Toolkit

As you continue your journey, build your own small library of reminders — tools that anchor you when life starts to speed up again.

These could include:

- A gratitude journal
- Your "Freedom Equation" notes
- A small box of meaningful items you *chose* to keep
- Your written *Freedom Statement* from the end of this guide

Keep them visible. Revisit them often.

Let them serve as quiet proof that peace isn't found in *adding more*, but in *living true*.

Final Note

Every tool, book, or practice listed here is just that — a tool. None of them can give you what you already hold: your awareness, your choice, your ability to begin again.

Keep this truth close:

You don't need more information to change your life.

You just need more intention.

That's where real freedom lives.

About the Author

Rosemarie Williams is a speaker, author, and leadership coach  known for helping people simplify their lives — from the way they lead to the way they live. Drawing from her background in behavior, communication, and mindful leadership, she teaches that freedom isn't about having more — it's about learning to live with what truly fits.

Through her *Empower Your Journey* series and workshops, Rosemarie has inspired countless readers to declutter not only their homes but their habits, priorities, and perceptions of success. Her work bridges the practical and the personal, guiding others to find peace, purpose, and possibility through intentional simplicity.

When she isn't writing or speaking, you'll find Rosemarie outdoors with her dogs, enjoying the quiet balance she now teaches others to create.

www.ingramcontent.com/pod-product-compliance
Lightning Source LLC
Chambersburg PA
CBHW071833210526
45479CB00001B/116